CREATING A FAITH-FILLED
ENVIRONMENT BEFORE YOU SERVE

FRESH WIND

FOR WORSHIP LEADERS

ANDRE HUDSON

Book Cover & Layout by Damascus Creative

Published by Radiant Publishing

Paperback ISBN: 978-1-963922-21-9

First Edition | Printed in the United States

DEDICATION

To my parents, my first worship pastors, and my introduction to worship ministry.

To my wife Rachel, who didn't sign up to be a pastor's wife, but has become a critical partner in God's Kingdom and a beautiful worshiper who sits at His feet.

To my daughters Amaya, Olivia, and Avery—the kind of worshipers the Father is seeking and a daily inspiration for me to glorify Jesus.

TABLE OF CONTENTS

FOREWORD
by Greg Hendricks

In every movement of God, there's a moment before the moment—a quiet space where hearts align, faith is stirred, and heaven is invited in. For worship teams, that space is often the pre-worship gathering. Yet too often, we walk into it distracted, depleted, or just going through the motions.

That's why Fresh Wind for Worship Leaders is not just timely—it's necessary.

My brother and friend, Andre Hudson, has captured something powerful in these pages. He's taken what many often overlook—a few minutes before service—and turned it into a launching pad for spiritual equipping and breakthrough.

This is more than a devotional; it's a heart tool. A culture-builder. A thermostat that sets your faith before you step onto the platform to serve God.

As someone who's been around worship teams, creative ministries, and Sunday gatherings, I know how easy it is to prioritize performance over presence. But God is not after polish—He's after posture. This book is a call to that. A call to intentionality. To stillness. To postured faith.

Through years of worship and ministry experience, Andre has worked to create a tool that doesn't just fill time before gatherings—it fills hearts before the Lord.

Each devotional, prayer, insight, and conversation prompt is rooted in Scripture and enriched with personal insight and perspective from his own journey as a worship leader.

I know Andre's heart is to equip individuals and teams to posture themselves rightly before God as they desire to serve Him.

This book is a reminder: before we lead others into worship, we must first be led—by the Spirit, shaped by the Word, and connected to one another in love and expectation before the Lord.

If you're a worship leader, creative director, or anyone who stands on a platform to serve God, I urge you—embrace the insights in this resource. Let it lead you into deeper waters with practical tools and meaningful conversations.

Posture yourself in faith before you make a sound for the Lord. Because when worship teams are spiritually aligned, the atmosphere shifts—and what happens in the pre-worship gathering doesn't stay there. It flows into the sanctuary and transforms lives.

Lead others to God from the overflow of your closeness with Him—and with each other.

It truly is one of our greatest privileges.

—Pastor Greg Hendricks

PREFACE

In the solitude of an Oceanside California hotel room in January 2025, I found myself in deep prayer about the future. In that stillness, the Lord planted the seed for this devotional—a thought that had never before crossed my mind. He revealed not only the chapters but the very purpose this work would serve. I felt awe, gratitude, and excitement at being entrusted with such a calling.

For fifteen years, I've served as a Worship Pastor in diverse church environments—from humble beginnings with eighteen people to San Diego's largest mega-church.

As a songwriter, producer, and teaching pastor, I've witnessed a universal challenge in our faith: falling into comfortable repetition. The worship community knows this struggle intimately.

Too often, we approach the platform from tradition rather than Biblical awareness. I've lived this reality firsthand.

This devotional emerges from that recognition—a weekly companion designed to deepen the spiritual roots of worship leaders and their teams. Each week offers an opportunity to reconnect with the Biblical foundations of worship, moving beyond the mechanics of music into the heart of what it means to lead God's people into His presence with great Biblical intention.

My prayer is that these pages become a Kingdom resource for any worship leader in any context, whether leading thousands or gathering with a small group in a living room.

As you journey through these devotionals week by week, I suspect you'll witness a transformation—not just in how you lead worship, but in how your team embodies worship.

May you see your community grow in biblical understanding, passion, love, and conviction. May you learn together how to "stir one another up to love and good works" (Hebrews 10:24).

In essence, may each person discover how to set the faith temperature of whatever environment they find themselves worshiping in, whether public or private.

Worship isn't just Sunday mornings—it's a lifestyle permeating every aspect of our being. It's cultivating a heart beating in rhythm with God's, hands serving with His compassion, and voices declaring His truth authentically. This devotional nurtures that holistic understanding, equipping you to lead with both musical excellence and spiritual depth.

Each week, you'll find Scripture passages to meditate on, reflections to consider, practical applications for your team, and prayer prompts to guide your conversations with God. Engage with these materials as invitations to encounter the living God who calls us to worship Him in spirit and truth.

I want to acknowledge first and foremost God, who has faithfully kept His promises for a hope and future in my life. "May the words of my mouth and the meditation of my heart be pleasing in Your sight, O LORD, my Rock and my Redeemer" (Psalm 19:14).

I extend my deepest gratitude to my wife of 19 years, Rachel, who is truly my best friend, co-laborer, and beautiful gift from God. Together, we've been blessed with three amazing daughters—Amaya, Olivia, and Avery—who are the pride of my life. Their support and understanding during the creation of this devotional has been invaluable.

I also want to thank my parents for their love, care, and intentionality in raising me. Their example of faithful service has shaped my understanding of what it means to worship God with one's whole life.

There are countless relationships for which I am thankful, and as you read these words, I pray you know how deeply you are loved by me and our family. More importantly, I pray you experience anew the transformative love of the Father who calls us to worship.

May this devotional serve as a faithful companion on your worship journey, sparking fresh passion and biblical insight week after week.

As we grow together in understanding what worship truly means, may we learn to create faith-filled environments wherever we go, offering praise that grows ever more pleasing to the One who is worthy of all our adoration.

In His service,

Andre

INTRODUCTION

Have you ever gathered with your team before a service and felt like you were just going through the motions? Slipping into routine with little to no real expectation of encountering God?

If so, you're not alone. Many worship teams find themselves in this place—distracted, disconnected, or simply lacking the faith and focus needed to lead others into God's presence. This book serves as a catalyst for fresh wind in your worship team, a tool designed to unify your team in faith by first stirring individual faith.

As worshipers, we're called to lead others into God's presence, but how can we do that effectively if we ourselves are not spiritually aligned? Worship teams often consist of individuals with diverse backgrounds, experiences, and levels of spiritual maturity.

These differences, combined with life's distractions, can make it challenging to get on the same spiritual page before stepping onto the platform. Yet when a team unifies in faith and expectation, the atmosphere shifts, and true worship emerges.

This 15-week guide will help your team grow together spiritually, setting the "faith tone" during your pre-worship team time before each service. It's designed to stir fresh wind into cold, distracted environments, creating passionate and faith-filled atmospheres. "But without faith it is impossible to please Him..." (Hebrews 11:6).

By applying these principles, individuals and teams will transition from reflecting whatever spiritual climate surrounds them to becoming vessels who usher in fresh wind and create faith-filled environments wherever they go.

Here's how this transformation happens. The book follows a five-part format centered around key topics to help build faith and unity within your team:

1. Leaders Insight – Provides insight into the day's devotional, helping leaders understand and guide the spiritual growth of the team. I would encourage you to also review the previous week's conversation.

2. The Devotional – Provides a faith-building message that lays the foundation for the team's focus and spiritual posture.

3. Team Reflection – Provides thought-provoking questions designed to spark personal reflection and collective discussion, activating individual and team faith.

4. Guided Prayer – Provides a faith-filled prayer to unify the team in agreement with the Biblical truth discussed, setting the stage for a powerful time of worship.

5. Personal Reflection – Gives team members space to actively engage in the faith journey. Since there's typically little time before a service starts, not everyone will get a chance to share. As you shepherd your team, you can follow up with members later. Or if you're involved in multiple services, you can continue the conversation, building on each other's faith.

These weekly devotionals are designed to be shared during your pre-service team gatherings, creating a consistent rhythm of spiritual alignment before ministering together. I recommend setting aside 15-20 minutes for each devotional to allow enough time for meaningful discussion and prayer, ideally incorporating this practice into your regular rehearsal schedule.

My prayer is that this book becomes a catalyst for transformation within your worship team. As you journey through these devotionals together, may you experience deeper faith, stronger unity, and greater expectation for God to move powerfully throughout your worship services.

Let's move beyond routine and step into a culture of faith that ignites passion and leads others into life-changing encounters with God.

WEEK 1
In Spirit and Truth

"But the hour is coming, and now is, when the true worshipers will worship the Father in spirit and truth;" —John 4:23

Leader's Insight:
The strategy of today's devotional is to encourage heart alignment by stirring a faith conversation about what God's word says about worship and how we are to approach Him. As everyone becomes more aligned in their understanding, they will approach the platform in greater unity in the faith.

Devotional: Beyond Comparison
If we visited 50 different churches, we might hear 50 different goals for the worship service. "We want high energy." "Just be passionate and remove distractions." Or worse—treating worship merely as a space filler until the message. Yikes! But the truth is that these human perspectives, whether good or misguided, ultimately do not matter.

What God says about worship matters. Paul warns in 2 Corinthians 12, "For we dare not class ourselves or compare ourselves with those who commend themselves. But they, measuring themselves by themselves, and comparing themselves among themselves, are not wise."

How often do we see this in Christian culture? We sing songs because they're popular or because our favorite worship team just released them. We feel pressured to write or perform in certain ways because that's what "success" looks like.

These things aren't inherently wrong, but when our motives become rooted in comparison rather than revelation, we risk operating in a different spirit altogether.

This was one of the issues the woman at the well had when she encountered Jesus. In John 4, Jesus goes out of his way to bring a kingdom reality to a woman (and ultimately a whole people group) who, despite having a lifestyle that wouldn't necessarily be identified as being "set apart," had some thoughts on the topic of worship for Jesus.

Her thoughts were rooted in her people's traditions, stating, "Our fathers worshiped on this mountain, and you Jews say that in Jerusalem is the place where one ought to worship."

Jesus graciously responds, "...You worship what you do not know...the true worshipers will worship the Father in spirit and truth..." This passage shows us that we can attempt to worship God with no understanding. And that kind of worship is not what He is "seeking."

Jesus's revolutionary answer to the woman invites us to move beyond locations and traditions into a deeper understanding of authentic worship. So what does it mean to worship God in Spirit? I believe it means that we must draw near to God not in physical rituals but in faith at the heart level.

What does it mean to worship God in truth? I believe that this requires us to worship God in agreement with what His word says. Also to worship Him in honesty and authenticity of heart. Let us worship God today not based on others' perceived offerings but from our own faith reservoir of love for Jesus!

Team Reflection:
Think about the lyrics of today's songs. How much of it can you relate to?
What parts, if any, have you not experienced in your own life?
How do you balance your "doing for God" with your "being with God"?

Prayer:
"Thank You Father that You are seeking worshipers who will worship in the spirit. Because You are spirit, help us to worship in the Spirit. We thank You for Truth. God, expand our revelation today according to Your Word on how You would like us to boldly approach Your throne. Amen."

Personal Reflection:

_____

_____

_____

_____

_____

_____

_____

_____

_____

_____

_____

_____

WEEK 2
Passion Is Not Enough

"...we did not consult Him about the proper order." 1 Chronicles 15:13

Leader's Insight:
In this devotional, we want to recognize how easily we can slip into executing ministry through mere repetition rather than true understanding. We can help our team see that even though we've led worship countless times and feel confident about how things will unfold, we might miss something crucial: there's a way that seems right to us, and then there's the way God has already expressed for worship to be carried out.

Devotional: Beyond Good Intentions
What a blessing it is to be able to serve in the house of God and lead His people to draw near to Him. If you are like me, I have led worship in different types of service thousands of times. From home groups, missions trips and beach baptisms to conferences and Sunday services. There is never a shortage of the demand on the worshiper.

In this familiarity we might unintentionally assume that our passion for the ministry, excellence of execution, and experience are all that is needed for our allotted time.

One of our greatest examples of a worshiper in Scripture is King David. There is an account in 1 Chronicles 13 where David is bringing the ark, which hosted the presence of God, back to Jerusalem. He had it in his heart to bring the nation together for a massive "worship event" as they ushered the presence of God into the city. He pitched the idea to the local leaders saying, "If it seems good to you, and if it is of the Lord our God …. for we have not inquired at it (the ark) since the days of Saul."(1 Chronicles 13:2 -3)

At first glance this seems like it would be a good idea to any one of us. I believe many times we gather together with our leaders and come up with plans that "seem good to us" and often forget to "inquire of the Lord" on the what, when, why, how and maybe even should.

Let's read on. They begin the worship service of the relocation of the ark and it says starting in verse 8: "Then David and all Israel played music before God with all their might, with singing, on harps, on stringed instruments, on tambourines, on cymbals and with trumpets."

I don't know when the last time you worshiped God "with all your might" and what that would even look like, but to me this expression says "passionate!" As they are worshiping the oxen pulling the cart with the ark on it stumbles. Uzza in a natural reaction reaches to keep the ark from falling and gets struck dead by The Lord! We all have had moments in worship we would like to forget but it is unlikely anyone died because of your missed musical note.

It says that David was upset with God but more importantly in verse 12 it says "David was afraid of God that day."

In all of our planning, excellence, good intentions and passion, I believe it is more important to have a healthy reverence and clear understanding of executing what God actually desires.

David, after inquiring what God requires, realizes that God's presence (the Ark) was never supposed to be carried by a convenient vehicle (an oxen) but it was to be carried on the shoulders of priests (the Levites). They moved the ark to Obed-Edom's home for 3 months until they could figure out what God's will was. In that time God blessed Obed-Edom and "all that he had."

As a side note, I believe it is important to be hosting God's presence in your home privately before you ever attempt to host it publicly.

We see in Chapter 15 that David wisely consults God about "the proper order" of things which starts with:

- Sanctification of the Levites (The ones responsible for ushering in the Presence) (1 Chronicles 15:12)

And then moves on to:

- Carry the ark on your shoulders (1 Chronicles 15:15)
- Play music skillfully (1 Chronicles 15:22)

In verse 26 we see that God comes and partners in the worship service by helping the Levites carry His presence. Isn't that the true goal of our meeting today? That in His proper order, we would worship Him and in His approval He comes in partnership?

Passion Is Not Enough

Team Reflection:
What does it look like to host His presence in your home?
How do you sanctify yourself before the worship meeting?
How can we partner today with Holy Spirit and carry His presence?

Prayer:
"God, we thank you that we do not have to strive to figure out how we should worship You for You have already determined the proper order. Because of the accomplishment of Jesus, You now call us a Royal Priesthood. Holy Spirit we ask that You would help us carry Your presence as we lead others to bring their offerings. Amen."

Personal Reflection:

_____

_____

_____

_____

_____

_____

_____

_____

_____

_____

_____

_____

_____

_____

_____

_____

_____

WEEK 3
Discomfort Is Welcome

"And without faith it is impossible to please God," —Hebrews 11:6

Leader's Insight:
The goal is to help our team grow increasingly comfortable with challenging biblical situations and topics. This includes our pre-worship team conversations and taking "faith risks" during our time on the platform. As we release our tendency to control every aspect of our gatherings, we'll witness more of God's potential and desires unfold in our meetings!

Devotional: Faith Over Feelings
When someone works out, they intentionally put their body through discomfort to achieve a desired result—better health. The same principle applies to our spiritual concepts. As we step into the fresh wind of God's word in areas that feel unfamiliar, our faith grows deeper and stronger.

Most of the world operates on feelings, emotions, and experience alone. As Christians, we shouldn't be content letting this remain true in our lives. As believers, we can't afford to also be unbelievers. What I mean is this: while our feelings and experiences matter, they shouldn't be our ultimate reality or guide.

As we take this faith journey together as a team, we want to keep believing God's word until our experiences align with it—not bring what we believe about God's word down to match our current experiences.

We'd all love to see the lyrics we sing in our churches come alive in our daily lives. When we sing about God's love, we want to actually experience His love. If we're singing that He's a miracle worker, we want to testify to real miracles! And if we sing "Holy Spirit come," we don't fight against Him when He actually shows up!

So how will we get there together? We'll practice getting comfortable with the uncomfortable biblical themes we don't yet understand. As we bring consistency to these areas, healthy familiarity will follow.

At the same time, we want to grow dissatisfied with our own ignorance and the status quo. God's goal has never been our comfort—it's that we would grow in the likeness of His son Jesus!

Team Reflection:
What spiritual topic makes you think, "I wish I knew more about that?"

What's your next step in faith and how can we help you grow in that area?

Prayer:
"God, if it is impossible to please You without faith, then let every action, thought and motive be full of faith! God, in the areas I struggle, I ask you to help my unbelief. I trust You, God, that You are faithful to finish the work that You have started in me. Amen."

Personal Reflection:

_____

_____

_____

_____

_____

_____

_____

_____

_____

_____

_____

_____

_____

_____

_____

Discomfort Is Welcome

WEEK 4
God's Goal for Our Meetings - Part 1

"What then shall we say, brothers and sisters? When you come together..."
—1 Corinthians 14:26

Leader's Insight:
Today's meeting aims to help our teams discover that the Word of God has already revealed what we should do when we gather together. We want to activate their faith by intentionally aligning ourselves with scripture every time we meet.

Acknowledge upfront that many of these concepts may be new, but challenge the team to commit to this faith journey together. Make yourself available to shepherd any questions or concerns your team might have, and lean on other leaders in your community to help the team grow.

Devotional: Scripture-Based Gatherings
Would it surprise you to learn that the Bible already tells us exactly what we should be doing when we gather as a team? In a world where people are led by "my truth," thank God the Bible speaks about "The Faith" (Jude 1:3, Ephesians 4:5).

What we're instructed to do when we come together is clearly laid out in 1 Corinthians 14:26:

"What then shall we say, brothers and sisters? When you come together, each of you has a hymn, or a word of instruction, a revelation, a tongue or an interpretation. Everything must be done so that the church may be built up." (NIV)

Example Goals:
- Share a song the Lord has placed on your heart
- Share what you sense the Lord is currently doing or saying
- Share a revelation the Lord has given you
- Prophesy and pray together in the Holy Spirit
- Interpret tongues for further direction

The Result:
The Church—your team—is built up in the Faith!

If you want to have faith-filled meetings that stir faith-filled team members, then you will need to be full of boldness, courage and faith.

"But without faith it is impossible to please Him, for he who comes to God must believe that He is, and that He is a rewarder of those who diligently seek Him." (NKJV)

In my experience (mostly within Western Church culture), Christians often believe in Jesus but struggle to believe in the things Jesus believed in. This happens because we're driven by our own limited experiences instead of God's limitless possibilities found in His Word.

Take Jesus' beliefs about healing the sick, cleansing lepers, raising the dead, and driving out demons (Matthew 10:7-8). If you're like me, you didn't grow up with any understanding of these things, and you certainly didn't experience, hear about, or participate in this type of ministry. `But I've discovered that just beyond our fear lies greater boldness and faith.

To become a thermostat—someone who sets the spiritual temperature—rather than a thermometer that simply reflects whatever happening in the environment around us, we need both boldness and faith.

Let's commit together from this point forward: when we gather, we won't just believe in Jesus, but we'll also believe in what He believed in! (John 14:12)

Team Reflection:
How do you feel about these goals for our meetings as outlined in 1 Corinthians 14?

Are you committed to being a "seeker of God's truth" and growing together as we align ourselves with God's Word?

What has the Lord revealed to you this week?

Prayer:
"Jesus, we thank You that You are good. We thank You that You are safe and trustworthy to believe. We are all here together because of our desire to please You and love You. Your perfect love casts out all fears we might have. We ask You for greater love, greater boldness, and that You would increase our faith. Amen."

Personal Reflection:

_____

_____

_____

_____

_____

_____

_____

_____

_____

_____

_____

_____

_____

_____

_____

_____

_____

WEEK 5
God's Goal for Our Meetings - Part 2

"Do not merely listen to the word, and so deceive yourselves. Do what it says." —James 1:22

Leader's Insight:
This devotional builds on last week's conversation. Your goal is to hear how the team has been processing what we discussed and help everyone recommit to walking together into all God is calling us to—first as believers, then as worship ministers.

Make yourself available to shepherd any questions or concerns your team might have. Don't hesitate to bring in other leaders from your community to help the team grow.

Devotional: Scripture-Based Gatherings
As we continue to grow together, it's crucial that information doesn't just stay in our heads but travels down to our hearts and gets put into action. James 1:22 warns us, "Do not merely listen to the word, and so deceive yourselves. Do what it says."

I believe you truly don't "know" something until you've experienced it yourself—with the goal of eventually leading others into their own encounters.

For example, I could read countless books about World War I and II, Vietnam, and the Iraq war. But if I approached a combat veteran and tried to relate to their experience, it would come across as offensive and tone-deaf. As we unpack last week's topic, let's step out in faith and spend most of our time putting into practice what we learned.

Recap on 1 Corinthians 14 (Activation)
- Share a song the Lord has placed on your heart
- Share what you sense the Lord is currently doing or speaking
- Share a revelation the Lord has given you
- Prophecy and pray together in the Holy Spirit
- Interpret tongues for further direction

The goal is to activate spiritual practices. A key indicator of maturity in any Biblical theme is your ability to not only demonstrate the topic but also teach and activate others to do the same! 1 Corinthians 4:20

Team Reflection:
What encouraged you during our time together today?

Where does your understanding need to align better with God's Word?

Prayer:
"God, we thank You that You are the Author and Finisher of our faith. We thank You that since we are never to plateau in our walk, our faith journey remains exciting. We eagerly desire all that You have for us and we pray that as we take the platform, the motives and meditations of our hearts would be pleasing to You. Amen."

Personal Reflection:

_____
_____
_____
_____
_____
_____
_____
_____
_____
_____
_____
_____
_____
_____
_____
_____
_____
_____

WEEK 6
The Opposition to Worship

"...we take captive every thought to make it obedient to Christ."
—2 Corinthians 10:3-6

Leader's Insight:
Today's goal is to recognize the many opportunities we have to become distracted during worship. We want to come together, identify these distractions, and actively shift our focus away from ourselves and back onto Jesus.

Devotional: Disarming Distractions
Would it be fair to say that if true worship requires us to be "God-conscious," then "self-consciousness" could never produce pure worship? If you're like me, you have an incredible ability to get distracted. Leading worship in a congregational setting usually means juggling multiple thoughts at once.

What time do I need to be on stage?
What key is the first song in?
Why is it so cold in here?
What are the lyrics again?
I need to play my instrument with excellence.
Why did my mix change?
The soprano is singing the wrong note.
Why did the pastor just walk up on stage?

These distractions don't even include what happens before you walk in.

Maybe you didn't get enough sleep, or you're feeling under the weather. Worse yet, you might be leading worship while walking through one of life's valleys. It's actually a minor miracle that we get through our worship gatherings considering the countless things that could derail us.

The truth is that all these distractions carry a level of self-consciousness. But here's the good news: we can disarm every one of these distractions through thanksgiving and staying answer-conscious.

When we simply apply truth, we'll see our flesh crucified and God-consciousness return to our worship.

Team Reflection:
What distractions are we facing today?

Have someone read Galatians 5:24, 2 Corinthians 10:3-6, and Isaiah 26:3.

Which Biblical truths from these passages can we apply to overcome these distractions?

Prayer:
"Jesus, You are the guest of honor in today's gathering. Right now we take every thought and every distraction captive and make it obedient to You. Thank You for Your Shalom. Your Spirit that breaks chaos. Thank You for truth. It indeed makes us free. Be glorified today in our undistracted worship. Amen."

Personal Reflection:

_____
_____
_____
_____
_____
_____
_____
_____
_____
_____
_____
_____
_____
_____
_____
_____
_____

The Opposition to Worship

WEEK 7
Break Religion

"... unless we "receive the kingdom as a little child," —Luke 18:17

Leader's Insight:
Today's invitation is to explore creative ways to challenge our thinking about what worship time could look like. This "challenge" should begin in the pre-worship team time or as early as possible. Much of this comes through giving ourselves permission to "play" or take risks in His presence. Breaking religious tendencies often means intentionally shaking up the day's possibilities!

Devotional: Permission To Play
As people, we're creatures of habit. We wake up, grab our coffee, and spend time in devotion. We take the same route to church and sit in the same section every week. We even stick to our familiar church vocabulary. We love our routines because they give us control. But what would happen if we released that control and opened ourselves to God's possibilities?

In Luke 18:16-17, Jesus tells his disciples that unless we "receive the kingdom as a little child," we will "by no means enter it." As a leader, this is a sigh of relief from my attempts in striving to reach heaven myself and pull others to follow. Children don't carry the weight of responsibility.

My kids never worry about paying bills or whether they'll eat today. In their healthy state, they trust completely, enjoy being with me, and look for ways to have fun.

When we look for opportunities to be bold or simply have fun in our services, freedom and joy often follow. Who wouldn't want their services overflowing with more freedom and joy?

I love watching people contemplate, "This is different! I'm not sure about this. But now that I think about it, there's nothing wrong or unbiblical about what's happening." This begins dismantling religious thinking.

Here are real examples of things I've done in pre-worship gatherings or during services:

- Have everyone share their most embarrassing worship experience.

- Get the congregation to not just clap but see if they can follow me in different time signatures, like Simon Says. (They never master the dotted eighth note.)

- Set my guitar down and dance.

- Lead worship stretches when the worship service begins and it feels "sleepy." I'll have the band loop an intro while I literally lead the congregation in stretching like we're back in elementary school P.E. Just 40 seconds does the trick.

Most of these childlike risks happen spontaneously. Not every faith risk needs humor. I often invite someone from the worship team to share what they sense the Lord is saying in a worship moment. When we have multiple services, rarely do two look identical. The goal isn't reckless unpredictability but bold enough faith to "let the children come to Him."

Team Reflection:
What religious habits or practices are part of your daily routine?

Who on our team brings the most joy and energy, and what makes them so fun to be around?

What is the most embarrassing thing you have experienced in a worship setting?

Prayer:
"God, now that we have planned and prepared ourselves to lead others into Your presence, help us not to forget to have fun. In Your presence is the fullness of joy. Show us what it looks like to delight ourselves in You today. Amen."

Personal Reflection

_____
_____
_____
_____
_____
_____
_____
_____
_____
_____

Break Religion

WEEK 8
Your Testimony Is a Weapon

"Let the redeemed of the Lord tell their story..." —Psalm 107:2

Leader's Insight:
Today's devotional aims to empower your team by helping them recognize something they already possess: their testimony in Jesus. During this sharing time, you'll explore how testimonies "destroy the works of the devil." As team members listen to each other's stories, they'll grow closer together—transparency creates powerful bonds that unite us.

Devotional: Tell Your Story
What I love about our testimony is that no one can tell you the things the Lord did in your life didn't happen. Our testimony in Jesus can become one of the greatest activators for connecting our faith to our ministry activities.

Revelation 12:11 shows us how believers overcome: "And they overcame him (the devil) by:

- The blood of the Lamb (Jesus's redemptive work in our lives)

- By the word of their testimony (what God has done in and through your life)

- And they did not love their lives to the death." (God's will above all else)

When we share our testimony, it actively combats the enemy in the hearer's life. "Faith comes by hearing." Our testimony brings encouragement, hope and faith, breaking off "works" that may be keeping others in bondage.

Even if the hearer hasn't experienced your realities themselves, they can know that what God has done in and through your life, they can also experience since "God does not show favoritism" (Romans 2:11).

In our worship today, I encourage you to recall what the Lord has done and what He continues to do in your life. As you play, sing or serve in whatever role you have, begin to attach your own testimony to the song.

Pay close attention to the shift in worship as you step out in faith and begin to prophesy, declare and proclaim the songs!

Team Reflection:
When did you first encounter Jesus?

How has your life changed since that encounter?

Which song from our set resonates with you most, and why?

Prayer:
"Jesus, when we were not looking for you and when we least expected it, You came and saved us! I thank you that You have given me a testimony. I thank you that today as we worship You, I will remind myself again of how great Your faithfulness has been toward me. Amen."

Personal Reflection:

_____

_____

_____

_____

_____

_____

_____

_____

_____

_____

_____

_____

_____

_____

_____

_____

_____

Your Testimony Is a Weapon

WEEK 9
Not in My Own Strength

"...My strength is made perfect in weakness." —2 Corinthians 12:9

Leader's Insight:
Today's challenge for the team is to recognize that we won't be striving to reach Him through our own efforts, but instead yielding our will to His will. We'll accomplish this by acknowledging that while preparedness and excellence remain essential, the true "power" doesn't come from our own abilities—it comes from God.

Devotional: Divine Power
I love the testimonies in the Bible of Jesus going out and preaching the gospel of the Kingdom in the synagogues. Wherever He went, He taught—but it wasn't just teaching. The supernatural accompanied Him. He healed the sick and cast out demons as well (seen in all four gospels). The people were blown away not only by His teaching but by the authority they recognized in Him.

There's no way anyone would ever be "bored at church" if signs and wonders like these happened regularly in our services. And guess what? They should be a regular occurrence. 1 Corinthians 4:20 says, "For the kingdom of God is not in word but in power." Again in 1 Thessalonians 1:5: "For our gospel did not come to you in word only, but also in power, and in the Holy Spirit."

So what does this mean for us as the worship leg of this operation? In Zechariah 4:6, the word of the Lord came to Zerubbabel: "Not by might nor by power, but by My Spirit,' says the Lord of hosts." Zerubbabel was leading the rebuilding of the temple when he received this reminder that success would come through divine empowerment, not human effort.

This same truth applies to us today. No matter how talented we are or how well we present our gifts, if God doesn't show up to the meeting, our gathering has missed the mark. In our own strength, no one gets saved, healed, or delivered. But "in Him" all things are possible!

Team Reflection:
What does it look like to yield to God's power in your worship role today?

What aspects of our church gathering are supernatural—things we can't manufacture on our own?

Prayer:
"God, give us a distaste for church activities that we can accomplish without Your power. God, increase our faith and hunger to boldly move not just in word but in deed. All for the glory of Jesus, Amen."

Personal Reflection:

_____

_____

_____

_____

_____

_____

_____

_____

_____

_____

_____

_____

_____

_____

_____

_____

_____

Not in My Own Strength

WEEK 10
The Cost

"I will not offer burnt offerings to the Lord my God that cost me nothing"
—2 Samuel 24:24

Leader's Insight:
This conversation aims to help us reflect on the different seasons we experience in life and discover how we can worship God through each one.

Devotional: Broken Spirit, Contrite Heart
"And Abraham said to his young men, 'Stay here with the donkey; the lad and I will go yonder and worship, and we will come back to you.'" Genesis 22:5.

In the testimony above, we see Abraham's willingness to sacrifice something precious to him without knowing the outcome, yet trusting God completely. True worship requires sacrifice. And not all sacrifices carry the same weight! We're all gathered here in the same physical space, but we're not all in the same spiritual place. Life brings peaks and valleys, and it's safe to assume that different spiritual elevations are represented even in this room. It's often easier to worship God on the mountaintop, but I believe it's more costly—and more valuable—when offered in life's valleys.

In 2 Samuel 12, we see King David fasting and praying desperately for his son's life to be spared. When his son dies, here's David's response: "So David arose from the ground, washed and anointed himself, and changed his clothes; and he went into the house of the Lord and worshiped."

We also see a different kind of offering in Mark 12:

"Now Jesus sat opposite the treasury and saw how the people put money into the treasury. And many who were rich put in much. Then one poor widow came and threw in two mites, which make a quadrans. So He called His disciples to Himself and said to them, 'Assuredly, I say to you that this poor widow has put in more than all those who have given to the treasury; for they all put in out of their abundance, but she out of her poverty put in all that she had, her whole livelihood.'"

I encourage you today: whatever chapter of life you find yourself in, seize the opportunity to bring a personal, sacrificial offering. This side of heaven will be your only chance to do so.

"For You do not desire sacrifice, or else I would give it; You do not delight in burnt offering. The sacrifices of God are a broken spirit, A broken and a contrite heart—These, O God, You will not despise." Psalm 51:16-17

Team Reflection:
Share a testimony about what God is doing in your life so we can celebrate together!

Share something we can pray with you about.

Prayer:
"Jesus, we thank You that in every occasion of life You can be worshiped. Today we tell our circumstances to bow to the name of Jesus. We thank You that there will be a day where there is no more death and no more crying. Let today be a continuation of worship until we get there. Amen."

Personal Reflection:

_____

_____

_____

_____

_____

_____

_____

_____

_____

_____

_____

_____

_____

_____

_____

_____

_____

The Cost

WEEK 11
The Journey

"...whose hearts are set on pilgrimage." —Psalm 84:5-7

Leader's Insight:
In this conversation, we'll explore how we can come together and journey collectively toward entering His presence. We'll accomplish this by reflecting on the Old Testament rituals of the Tabernacle of Meeting and meditating on what these spiritual principles mean for us today. We'll break this down simply into three areas: the "Outer Court," the "Holy Place," and "The Holy of Holies."

Devotional: Broken Spirit, Contrite Heart
Sometimes it's challenging for us to come together, worship, and enter God's presence. You might have heard it said: "You can't take others somewhere that you're not going."

While many worshipers do not need someone else to help them connect with God, this rings true more often than not. Honestly, it's better when we make the worship journey together without losing anyone along the way!

In the Old Testament, the Israelites set up a Tabernacle or "Tent of Meeting" where people could worship God and bring their sacrifices and offerings. They had specific stations in this meeting place with practices they performed as acts of worship. Let's look at three locations in the tent and use them to guide our reflection and prayer before we worship together.

The Outer Court

Psalm 100:4 says to "Enter His gates with thanksgiving and His courts with praise: give thanks to Him and praise His name." Thankfulness is such a powerful Kingdom principle. Being grateful brings proper perspective. When we voice our thankfulness, lesser cares and concerns fall into their rightful place.

The outer court also housed the Laver—a bowl of water used for ceremonial washing before entering the holy place. This is where we acknowledge any sin and repent.

The Holy Place

As we continue our worship journey, we enter the Holy Place. Several items were found here, but let's focus on the candlestick. The fire on the candlestick represents the Holy Spirit. A candle needs to be lit to function. Before we minister to others, we want to be set on fire for the Lord! We should ask the Holy Spirit to anoint us for the task ahead.

The Holy of Holies

This is where the ark of the covenant resided. Inside the ark, God's manifest presence dwelt. In all our times of worship, regardless of the environment, God's presence is always the goal of our worship journey! As a verb, "tabernacle" means to dwell, abide, or take up residence. Once we realize God's presence today, let's dwell there!

Team Reflection:
What are you thankful for today?

Ask the Holy Spirit to reveal anything you need to repent for.

Spend time in worshiping and praying in the spirit before you lead today.

Prayer:
"God, we thank You for goodness and mercy. We thank You for sending Jesus. What a demonstration of Your love. We repent of our sins and thank You for continuing to transform us day by day. God, Your presence is the only goal of our meeting today. We pray that You would inhabit the praise of Your people! Amen."

Personal Reflection

_____

_____

_____

_____

_____

_____

_____

_____

_____

_____

WEEK 12
The Mighty Ones

"...You have come to thousands upon thousands of angels in joyful assembly, to the church of the firstborn, whose names are written in heaven." - Hebrews 12:22-24

Leader's Insight:
Today's meeting focuses on acknowledging that we aren't the center of attention in our worship gathering, nor are we alone. It's important to remember that God is present alongside other supernatural beings, including angels and more!

Devotional: Joining the Eternal Song
I once heard someone say that when we gather together, we never "begin" or "start" worship—we simply join it. We recognize that continuous worship flows around God's throne, never ceasing, never ending.

"Day and night they never stop saying: 'Holy, holy, holy is the Lord God Almighty, who was, and is, and is to come'" Revelation 4:8.

I wonder how often we pause to acknowledge that heavenly beings are present in our meetings—ministering angels with all the potential of their angelic activity! Our worship would never grow stale if we understood what they know about God and how He deserves to be worshiped.

I'm sure we've all witnessed this in worship meetings: someone engaging with hunger and passion while right next to them sits someone who couldn't appear more disinterested. It's a strange reality that in the same room, one person can be "washing the feet of Jesus" while their distracted neighbor misses that He was even there.

I wonder if we could bring a collective offering that would cause even the "Mighty Ones" to recognize and join in. "Praise the LORD, you his angels, you mighty ones who do His bidding, who obey His word." Psalm 103:20. Picture a Spirit-filled atmosphere where angelic activity fills the place where we gather—where things beyond our own strength happen as we lift the name of Jesus! "Are not all angels ministering spirits sent to serve those who will inherit salvation?" Hebrews 1:14

Team Reflection:
Have you ever wondered, "What's really happening in the room during worship?"

Have you ever felt a mysterious "touch" during worship that you couldn't quite explain?

Have you ever glimpsed "in the Spirit" the unseen activity around you?

Prayer:
"God, we thank you that today we get the amazing opportunity to join in with worship that was going on before we were here and will continue well after we are gone. We ask that You would activate our spiritual senses, giving us a greater awareness of Your Kingdom that has come on Earth as it is in Heaven! Amen."

Personal Reflection:

_____
_____
_____
_____
_____
_____
_____
_____
_____
_____
_____
_____
_____
_____
_____
_____

The Mighty Ones

WEEK 13
The God Outside of Time

"...With the Lord a day is like a thousand years, and a thousand years are like a day." —2 Peter 3:8

Leader's Insight:
This devotional aims to pull the team away from everyday distractions by focusing their attention on our partnership with biblical characters throughout worship history. This should spark conversations that help the worship team feel the weight and honor of joining with both history and eternity in worship.

Devotional: Transcending Time
Sometimes I think we forget that God exists outside the boundaries of time. This concept is often hard to grasp because everything we know gets measured by our understanding of time. It takes 365 days for our blue planet to orbit the sun. We know there are 24 hours in a day. But God isn't confined to these laws.

I once heard it explained this way: our human experience with time is like standing in the middle of a parade. We can remember where we started in the procession and glimpse a bit ahead, but we can't see very far in either direction. God, however, hovers above the parade like someone in a helicopter, able to view the beginning and end simultaneously!

Since this is true, God can actually be present throughout history, in the present with us today, and in the future all at once.

That means while we worship God together today, He can choose to be present with us while also being with Abel presenting his acceptable offering, with Abraham offering up Isaac, with David ushering the Ark back to Jerusalem, or with Mary pouring expensive perfume on Jesus' feet. He can watch the widow placing her two coins in the temple treasury while visiting a ten-day prayer meeting in the upper room with the first church. We get to bring our offering today and join our place in time within God's greater worship service.

It still blows my mind that David, when writing the Psalms, wrote under the prophetic guidance of the Lord. Then Jesus would later quote those same passages from Psalms that He had inspired David to write generations earlier! Wow! I challenge us today to align our hearts with Heaven in such a way that Jesus inhabits our worship meeting in our moment in history.

Team Reflection:
How do these biblical examples of worship compare to the offering we're bringing today? (Examples given: Abel, Abraham and Isaac, David, Mary, the widow, Jesus' followers in the upper room)

What would it look like for us today to align ourselves with the same heart posture as these examples?

Prayer:
"God, You are the One who inhabits the praises of Your people. Holy Spirit, help us today to bring an offering that is worthy of You visiting. Amen."

Personal Reflection:

_____
_____
_____
_____
_____
_____
_____
_____
_____
_____
_____
_____
_____
_____
_____
_____
_____
_____
_____

WEEK 14
Prophesy in Your Window

"Follow the way of love and eagerly desire gifts of the Spirit, especially prophecy." —1 Corinthians 14:1

Leader's Insight:
Today's devotional goal is to encourage and activate the ministry team to move beyond simply singing, playing, or producing worship. Instead, we want them to lean in and declare what God is saying through their unique roles and perspectives. We'll accomplish this by building a biblical understanding of what it means to prophesy and cultivating the boldness and faith needed to step into that prophetic space.

Devotional: Prophetic Musicians
Have you ever considered that the God who spoke everything into existence made us human beings in His image? (Genesis 1:3, 26-27) We're compatible with God—able to hear His voice and respond! He spoke things that were not as though they already existed, and we can do the same.

Here's the definition of prophecy that we'll use in our worship context: What is God saying or doing, and how can I express that biblically and appropriately in my role today?

When we worship, we participate in shifting the atmosphere because God inhabits the praises of His people (Psalm 22:3). And where God's Spirit is, there is freedom (2 Corinthians 3:17) (1 Corinthians 25:1) (1 Samuel 10:5-6) (1 Samuel 16)! Wouldn't it be amazing to partner with God in our worship service today in such a way that He would be glorified, inhabit our praises, and set people free? I've seen this happen before, and I'm sure it occurs more than we even realize.

In 1 Samuel 16:14-23, King Saul is tormented by an evil spirit, and David is brought in to play the harp. When David plays, the music soothes Saul, and the evil spirit leaves him. Do we think the evil spirit responded to David's excellent playing? Or because his song hit the top 5 on Christian radio? Maybe it was the infinite pad playing behind him, or because he prayed in tongues and anointed himself with oil beforehand?

No, I believe Saul's freedom came because David was anointed by God—not only ready to play skillfully, but also operating in his calling and playing with faith and conviction. I've witnessed this, and maybe you've personally experienced someone receiving deliverance and being completely transformed in God's presence during worship.

During our worship time, make sure you're looking and listening for opportunities to "pull the car over" and ask the Holy Spirit, "What are You saying and doing?" "How do You want me to respond or prophesy from my role in this moment?" The Bible encourages us to seek the gifts, especially the gift of prophecy (1 Corinthians 14:1).

A phrase we frequently use during our team prep sessions is "Don't fight it. Don't fake it." Let's agree to let the Holy Spirit be our worship director today.

Team Reflection:
From your role today, what would prophesying look like?

What are some possible outcomes if God shows up in today's meeting?

Prayer:
"God, we are grateful that You have given us our talents and gifts and allow us to give them back to You as an act of worship. Since You are always speaking, help us to perceive Your will and by faith attempt to respond. Amen."

Personal Reflection

_____

_____

_____

_____

_____

_____

_____

_____

_____

_____

_____

_____

_____

Prophesy in Your Window

WEEK 15
Casting Every Crown

"...'You are worthy, O Lord, to receive glory and honor and power;'"
—Revelation 4:10-11

Leader's Insight:
This topic aims to provide practical tools for combating self-focus, self-exaltation, and pride during our worship services.

Devotional: Give It All Back
Having gifts and talents is truly beautiful. Being able to use your God-given creativity to bless Him is extraordinary. And when He anoints someone's talents, it becomes clearly evident and exciting. However, platform ministry has a way of adding gasoline to the fires of ego. It presents a continuous call to "humble yourself in the sight of the Lord."

We're literally on a stage, but our goal as we worship is to help people see God, not us! We know that Satan was originally Lucifer, a high-ranking angel who most believe oversaw the worship of God.

In Ezekiel 28:16, when referring to Lucifer, it reads: "By the abundance of your trading (merchandise), you became filled with violence within, and you sinned; Therefore I cast you as a profane thing Out of the mountain of God; And I destroyed you, O covering cherub, From the midst of the fiery stones."

I want to highlight the word "merchandise" here. When something—in this case worship—gets merchandised, it's traded for gain or profit. Essentially, Satan wasn't allowing all of God's worship to pass through him. Instead, he was taking some of God's worship for himself! He was merchandising the worship.

"For you have said in your heart: 'I will ascend into heaven, I will exalt my throne above the stars of God... I will be like the Most High.'" Isaiah 14:13-14 Initially, I don't believe most people enter worship ministry with motives to draw attention to themselves. But performance culture definitely makes this challenge harder to navigate.

So how can we guard against this? In Revelation 4:10, we see the elders casting their crowns (their rewards) before God's throne. They understand that every good and perfect gift comes from heaven, so God alone deserves the glory!

One way I guard my heart is this: whenever something pulls me toward self-exaltation—a compliment from someone, a nice lick from my instrument, or a beautiful-sounding mix—I picture that thing as a crown. Then, with my imagination, I cast it at Jesus' feet! This practice has tremendously helped me keep the focus on the true focus of our gatherings: Jesus Christ.

Team Reflection:
What patterns have you noticed that pull you toward self-exaltation?

Picture that example as a crown and cast it at Jesus's feet.

Share strategies you use to guard your heart.

Prayer:

"Search me, O God, and know my heart; Try me, and know my anxieties; And see if there is any wicked way in me, And lead me in the way everlasting." (Psalm 139:23-24) I repent now for any time that I drew the focus off You and placed it on myself. Holy Spirit, help me today to present a holy and undefiled offering before You. Amen!"

Personal Reflection

_____
_____
_____
_____
_____
_____
_____
_____
_____
_____
_____
_____
_____
_____

Casting Every Crown

RECAP
Reflecting on Our Journey Together

"...are being transformed into the same image from glory to glory, just as by the Spirit of the Lord." —2 Corinthians 3:18

As we close this 15-week journey, let's pause and remember how far we've traveled together. We began by establishing that God seeks worshipers who worship Him in spirit and truth (Week 1), learning that passion alone isn't enough without Biblical understanding (Week 2). We embraced discomfort as a pathway to growth (Week 3), and discovered God's specific design for our gatherings (Weeks 4-5).

We've learned to recognize and overcome the opposition to worship (Week 6), break free from religious routine (Week 7), and wield our testimonies as weapons against the enemy (Week 8). We've acknowledged our dependence on Holy Spirit's power rather than our own strength (Week 9) and discovered how to worship God through every season and cost (Week 10).

Together we've journeyed through the tabernacle—from thanksgiving in the outer court to dwelling in God's presence (Week 11). We've opened our eyes to the mighty ones who join our worship (Week 12), recognized our place in worship history (Week 13), and stepped into prophetic ministry (Week 14).

Now, as we cast every crown at Jesus' feet, we complete this journey not as the same people who began 15 weeks ago, but as a team transformed by fresh wind—equipped to create faith-filled environments wherever we serve.

Feel free to go back and recycle the complete journey with your team to reinforce the new culture. People will often grow at different paces, so going back through over and over will never hurt. You can also try letting other trusted team members lead the conversations.

I pray that you have found great value in this Kingdom resource and that you have most importantly grown in your own walk with The Lord. If you have found value in this devotional, feel free to share it with other worship ministries in your town or city and let's believe together "the hour is coming, and is now here, when the true worshipers will worship the Father in spirit and truth, for the Father is seeking such people to worship him. God is spirit, and those who worship him must worship in spirit and truth."
(John 4:23-24)

Final Reflection Question:
How has our team's approach to worship changed since Week 1, and what will you carry forward from this journey?

Prayer:
"Father I thank You for this time of transformation alongside my brothers and sisters. I thank You that You are always growing me and taking me from glory to glory and strength to strength. Thank You for these few weeks where seeds were planted and were watered. I now trust You to bring the increase in my life & community for the glory of Jesus. Amen."

Personal Reflection:

_____

_____

_____

_____

_____

_____

_____

_____

_____

_____

_____

_____

_____

_____

_____

_____

_____

_____

LET'S STAY CONNECTED

Andre Hudson
thewindmillministry.com
thewindmillministry@gmail.com
@mrandre7000 (Instagram)

Music available on all major platforms

WNDMLL MSC
wndmllmsc@gmail.com
@wndmllmsc (Instagram, Facebook, YouTube)

Music available on all major platforms

Booking + Ministry Inquiries
Interested in booking Andre for:

- Worship Leading
- Speaking Engagements
- Worship Team Conference Calls

Email us: thewindmillministry@gmail.com

More Resources: Explore tools, music, and merch at The Windmill Store at thewindmillministry.com

We'd love to connect with you and hear how *Fresh Wind* is impacting your worship team! Share your stories and stay connected for future resources and encouragement.

www.ingramcontent.com/pod-product-compliance
Lightning Source LLC
Chambersburg PA
CBHW081722120626
46550CB00010B/3212